Pilgr

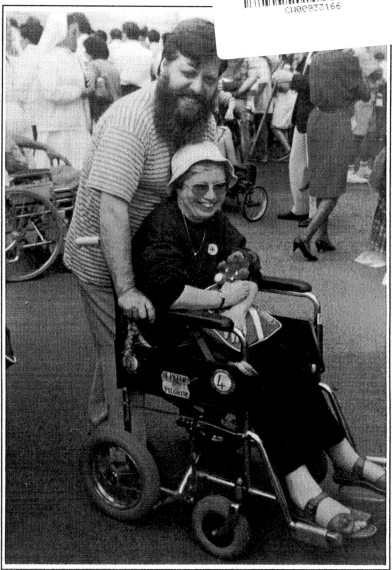

Pauline and Richard

PILGRIMS, PAULINE & RICHARD

PAULINE HARKESS

PILGRIMS, PAULINE & RICHARD

BY

PAULINE HARKESS

The Adelphi Press
4-6 Effie Road, London, SW6 1TD

Published by the Adelphi Press
Printed and bound in the U.K.
ISBN 1 85654 089 8

CHAPTER ONE

Christmas holidays are over. Weather-wise it is cold and windy. To give us a cheer-me-upper we browse through photographs taken last year on our first pilgrimage to Lourdes, France. Who are 'we' you ask. My husband, Richard and myself, Pauline. Just an ordinary married couple who wanted to do a pilgrimage. We've been married for nine years and wanted to celebrate the fact in an unusual way. Sickness is a part of our life, both of us have arthritis in our bodies. Neither of us allows this illness to bother us too much. I also had another illness but an operation put me better.

Back to this year. Where shall we go for a convalescent holiday? Without hesitation we choose Lourdes again. Why? Mm, hard to explain, so I won't try.

Richard hunted in our glory cupboard until he found the Roman Catholic newspaper we had been given the previous Sunday, at the united service of all three churches of different denominations in our village of Blackhall. We are not members of this church but sometimes attend their services.

In the paper there was an advertisement place by the tour operators we went with last year, Saint Peter's in London, and the phone number was included. Richard reads out the numbers while I dial, then, speaking to the lady at the other end, I ask to be sent this years brochure of tours to Lourdes.

Our local Methodist Superintendent helped us to find a tour which had a late vacancy we could take up, hence the London group. All we can do now is wait for the postman to call later in the week with our requested brochure.

Whoe! What a surprise, the brochure has arrived by this morning's post. It contains, however, last years information but the organizer has put a note with it saying if we book now we can go at last year's price, as this year's books are still at the printers. Us likes a bargain, so we sit ourselves down and discuss ways and means, as money is in short supply. We budget our cash for this each week, and what is left over will be put aside for our pilgrimage. May seems the best time for us as it will be our tenth anniversary present to each other. We like exploring. A packed programme is planned and everything is optional, so we will be able to choose out our outings. As I tire quickly, I've taken up the offer of a wheelchair from the tour organizer, to make moving more comfortable. Richard will be my pusher as well as the new friends we make. This type of pilgrimage is a friendly holiday, everyone helping one another.

It is early evening, the application form is filled in neatly. Richard has gone into the village on this wild and windy night to post off the envelope to catch the early morning post.

Check list (afterthought): have I put down our names correctly, made up the diet sheet, ordered the wheelchair, transport from London to Luton airport, planned how to get to London from Blackhall?

Next on the list is to join the Peterlee library and take out a French beginners' guide on 'words' helpful to the tourist. Talk, talk, that is what we have done all of today, planning what clothes to take, what we need to buy to freshen up our wardrobe. Have decide to travel light, just one medium sized suitcase between us will do. Past holidays always found us packing more than we needed; learning from this, we will only pack the bare items this time, clothes that match one another.

How time flies by, it is the end of January. The new flu caught us out. Now better. "French for Travellers" is being played as I type this. Keep trying, we've been told, repeat, replay, some words will stick in your mind. Will give it another try. Our accents are ******! A phrase book came with the tape so I am looking up Mister Rabbit, as my little ten penny toy will be going on its pilgrimage with us. (He travels free.) A little toy soon makes new friends with shy folk. Monsieur Lapin, that sounds just right for wee rabbit. I'll spend a couple of hours knitting him his holiday outfit. Along with Monsieur Lapin will be "Louie" a small teddy bear Richard bought for me last year in Lourdes. My other "Ted" found a new owner to live with last year whom he made friends with at the hotel.

Jesus answers prayers via a sister who has knitted us an Arran jumper each. Prayer plays a large part in our lives, both of us are Christians. We will take these jumpers with us.

CHAPTER TWO

Confirmation of our booking came today. We can go ahead with confidence, planning our pilgrimage holiday. It is February, brr, the wind howls, the rain lashes against the windows, we are cosily tucked up indoors, planning spring clothes. Our suitcase has been emptied of its storage contents and left in the spare room to await the chosen items to be packed.

Monsieur Lapin has his new outfit and will be clipped to the haversack which will take our sketching paper and pencils for our 'homework' on this book. Cameras will record what otherwise would be missed. Neatly folded inside one of the bags to make it easier to go through customs. A list of all that we carry will be in my purse for easy access, if needed.

I was born in small village in Cornwall, now a built up area. Bernadette Soubirous was born in a little village similar to mine, **Lourdes.** A sufferer of asthma , she missed a lot of schooling so had a lot of difficulty in the three R's - reading, writing, arithmetic. It was on February 11th 1858, while out collecting firewood with her sister and friend, by the side of the River Gave and village rubbish dump outside her village, Lourdes, that she first saw the vision of a "Beautiful Lady" in a niche in the rock. No-one believed her for some time, but gradually the priest and the villagers came to realize the little teenage girl was seeing and listening to someone in the or on the rock by the rubbish dump.

In all, eighteen visions were seen by the girl. Bernadette faithfully passed on the messages the "Beautiful Lady" asked her to relay to the people of Lourdes. One request was that a church/ chapel be built on that site. People were to come in procession for prayer and penance. The muddy water in which Bernadette washed herself at the bidding of her "Beautiful Lady" proved to be healing water. There are many books and articles written on this happening.

No-one leaves the shrine empty handed. Inner healing, outer healing have been proved to have taken place and people are blessed; every evening torchlight processions are well attended by locals and tourists alike, as they come together to do the bidding asked of them via Bernadette all those years ago.

CHAPTER THREE

Six weeks to go. It is Easter Sunday. For Richard and I, a very special day, as we were made members of our local chapel this morning at the 8am service. Thirteen folk gathered to welcome us into their midst with the service of Holy Communion. We all knelt together to give praise that Jesus had risen. We partook our breakfast together after the service. At our requests, we wanted a simple welcome. It was done so reverently by our minister.

Hotels are the next point to discuss. We have been trying to find overnight accommodation for the outward journey which offers an evening meal. So far, no luck. Will have to book our coach seats soon as it becomes busy with the tourist season beginning. Trying to make up our minds which way to travel to London. Will enquire at train station and coach, then choose the best one for us. The tour we are going on is the five-day four-night full board one, by air and coach. It is as follows:

Monday

12.45 pm - Coach departs from London for Luton airport; it leaves from outside Westminster Cathedral.

2.15 pm - Latest check-in time at International Luton airport.

3.50 pm - Flight to Lourdes. Hot lunch in flight.

6.35 pm - Land at Lourdes Airport where the coach awaits to take us to our hotels.

9.30 pm - Introductory visit to the Domain and Grotto under the guidance of the Pilgrim Spiritual Director who will open the pilgrimage in front of the Grotto.

Tuesday

8.30 am -   Mass (after our continental breakfast) followed by a "Sound and Slide" presentation, telling the story and explaining the meaning of Lourdes. Group visits and prayer at the Baths.

1.30 pm -   After lunch - walking tour of Lourdes in the steps of Saint Bernadette.

8.45 pm -   After supper - Torchlight procession.

Wednesday

9.00 am -   Mass (at the Grotto if possible) or international Mass; underground Basilica.

10.30 am - Stations of the cross (optional around the town or the Chapel).

Thursday

8.30 am -   Optional visit to Bartree, the farm where Saint Bernadette worked, the Parish Church, Mass, the sheep fold where she spent many hours minding the sheep. Return via the lake where we can buy refreshments.

12 noon   Lunch

2.00 pm   Closing of the pilgrimage in front of the Grotto.

5.15 pm   Coach calls to take us to the airport.

8.10 pm   Flight to London.

9.30 pm   London.

Note: France is one hour ahead of Britain.

Time for countdown on our wall calendar, and a check of all the details connected with our pilgrimage. Checklist: toiletries, clothes, tablets, passports, tickets, travel documents, doctor's note (just in case), timetables, traveller cheques, French francs, English money, ourselves.

Tuesday April 21st finds us in Sunderland City, wandering round the city visiting here and there, collecting information on transport to London. Joy, we came across one operator who does the coach plus an hotel for overnight stayers. Trouble is we will have to travel to Newcastle to book. Ah. Well, that will be another days outing next week. Slowly, everything is taking shape. The past few weeks we have been putting time aside to sit quietly to think and pray, an important part of preparing ourselves and significant for others who will be on the tour with us. Adventure, here we come.

Once more, a change in our planning. Through a friend we learned of a Salvation Army hotel in London which does B + B at a reasonable price. So we will stay there on going and coming back to Lourdes. Our 'food' we will buy as we want it. The coach is booked. All the tickets necessary for our journey now in our possession. Countdown: five days to go. These will be busy days as we tidy the house, cancel the milk etc,etc. Neighbours informed we will be away as they will keep an eye on the house. We are a friendly street.

FOOTNOTE:

I had a tooth out during this past week, by gas, no problem, but afterwards came down with an infection which has made me poorly in the throat, with earache plus blackouts and migraine. Went to the doctor's twice in a few days for help. They inspected, they talked, no antibiotics to be obtained although we almost begged for them; none was prescribed. PUZZLED! We are! However, we talked to each other and have decided to carry on with the pilgrimage. I was prescribed Solpadol, a pain killer, by the first doctor to ease the bruising on my chin caused by the extraction. Just thought I'd mention this as the pilgrimage will now be a real effort of "Faith."

Service in progress

The Grotto

River Gave

Remembrance Garden

Pauline

Richard

The Grotto

Pauline and "Ted"

Richard after his bath

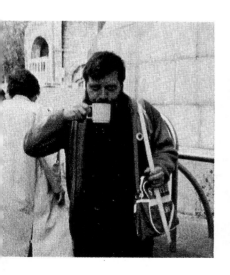

Drinking at the taps

Quick draw

Just looking?

Hospital

River Gave

Dead wood

Town "bus"

Richard
Right: Bascilla

Above: Church
Top Right: Richard and wheels
Far Right: Flowers at St. Joseph's Gate
Below: Awaiting the free bus to visit "City of the poor"

Mountain view

Sheperds Hut in mountain

Horse and pony rides to mountain slope

Mountain stream

Pyrénées Mountains
(also below)

CHAPTER FOUR

It is now the eve of our pilgrimage. Case is packed, labels written, tablets from the chemist are in our hand luggage, sandwiches and soft drinks plus straws, as I am a messy drinker when a vehicle is moving. Hotels leaflets checked, and the map of London. Salvation Army directions for our overnight stays. Everything is in order for tomorrow. Now to relax, have a bath, wash hair, then set the alarm clock for six am to give our bodies time to settle after breakfast, before the journey. Healthwise, I have lost my hearing almost completely, just muffled sounds come through, my speech is slurred after I try to hold a conversation with someone after a few sentences; but in *faith* we are going to Lourdes.

The awaited day is HERE! We are up and ready, watching TV while consuming toast and coffee. Weather is dull, cloudy, foggy, won't be too hot for travelling. We are glad there is no rush to prepare food etc., just relax waiting for the taxi to pick us up at nine am. Neither of us has slept much, still we will be able to have a nap on the coach later. Once more the house is checked, windows, doors all locked and secure.

Here is the taxi, right on time to take us to Peterlee. It only takes a few minutes to get to the bus station. We wait a while, standing by the bus stop, watching the world go by, not much to see on a Sunday morning, all is still. Other travellers are gathering around us. Our coach arrives, on we get, settle into our seats. The driver apologises to Richard as the tickets haven't arrived from another colleague, but off we go, collect the tickets when we change coaches (says the driver - news to us, the change-over). We are seated on the front seats, left hand side of the driver. A nice view. Monsieur Lapin has a canny view of himself, peeping out between the hostess's seat and the exit door. We stop to pick up passengers at Hartlepool, Middlesbrough, Stockton, Darlington; rain is falling quite heavily.

At Leeming Bar a smooth change-over is done. Och! We find they have only booked for one passenger, not two, so the ticket is altered, the mix-up fixed as the Blue Line offices are here. Seated this time third seat from the door, left-hand side. We choose this side of the coach so as to see the road signs clearly. It is interesting to see the miles get smaller as we near our destination, London.

The journey is pleasant, the rain stops, the sun shines. We are bang on time at Kings Cross. Richard spots the road we have to walk along, so we are soon at the hotel. Sign the visitors' book and get the key to the room. We leave our case in the room and go to explore.

Need feeding, notice several cafes as we walk up the road. We go back to Kings Cross to check on the local buses to Victoria station for tomorrow. Being a Bank Holiday it will be a Sunday service. This done, we visit a nearby cafe for a hamburger. Disaster here, Richard orders two plain burger, no sauce or onions. Tomato sauce I do not like, it makes me sick. However, the burgers come with everything in 'em so I separate the bottom halves and give Richard the rest to eat. An ad-lib tea, but the coffee is good.

Back at the hotel, sitting in the lounge, we chat to the others around us. Wow! The weather has turned into a scorcher at the end of the day. We feel overdressed, as when we left this morning it was raining and cold. We explored Kings Cross while we were out, we tell them, the underground was fascinating, stood watching people buying tickets from machines in the walls. We tried a chocolate machine but lost our money so bought a small bar each at a nearby shop. It was yukkie, all melted, sticky, gooey. Had to wash ourselves after this treat. Neither of us likes to spend money on the Sabbath but it was unavoidable as we needed to eat.

It has been a peaceful evening, now to retire to bed. We have set the travelling clock for seven a.m. This will allow time to get sorted and get the bus to Victoria/Westminster Cathedral Where we will catch the coach to Luton airport. What luxury last night, coffee in our room, an extra but worth it.

Eleven-fifteen p.m. I am taken poorly. For ten minutes I fight for breath, at Richard's suggestion I drink the last can of soft drink which we had left, slowly sipping through a straw. This makes me burp, which clears the congested lungs. Spent the rest of the night propped up on the bed while Richard dozed on his. Monday morning, six-thirty a.m., up and about, washed, bags organized. Weather is clammy, warm, sticky. Packed our jumpers, so it will be T -Shirt and slacks only to travel in comfort. Now to sit quiet for a bit, ready for the off. Each room has a bible, Good News Version, so together read Psalms twenty-five.

Bus fare money is at the ready, we noticed last night correct change only on the buses here, no change given. Tickets for London to Luton are also ready, makes for easy travelling if you are well-prepared beforehand.

Breakfast, fruit juice, cereal, fried egg and bacon, toast, tea, coffee - went down a treat. Not often we breakfast like this. Richard enquires of the staff our bus route into Victoria Station, Finds our research is accurate, seventy pence by bus, eighty pence by underground. Teapot holds four cuppas, coffee-pot three so we drain both pots.

Och! We be clots, thickheads. Walked in the wrong direction for thirty minutes looking for the cathedral, so we went back to the Victoria Station and asked directions only to find it was just around the corner. We get there. It is cool sitting under a hugh beach tree outside the cathedral. When we have cooled we will go inside the church just to sit and reflect. Richard has gone to a nearby shop to get us a cold drink each. Hydration will become a problem if we don't do something about it as the weather has become a "roaster." While on my own, just sitting, folk who are milling around me awaiting other tours, pass the time of day with me. The Saint Peter's Badge attracts them. This badge has its uses for this Christian.

English is the common language but folk here don't understand our speech. Richard asked for two tins of Coke, none available at this time of morning, all sold out, so he asked for two cartons

13

of milk. In the end he was given cardboard cups and the carton of milk which to them was just milk. It was straight from the fridge, very tasty and refreshing.

Now inside the church building. A mass is on so we sit very quietly as the service has almost ended. Walked around inside the building. Lots of side Chapels, all is peaceful.

One thirty p.m. Luton Airport. We were the only passengers from Victoria. It was a lovely ride. No hold-ups, took one hour. We are now in the airport lounge. Someone has helped me to wash my hands in the loo. I find taps difficult as I've no working muscles in my thumbs. It's a ways and means committee with myself to do simple things. "Trust in the lord and He will provide." I often repeat this to myself when harassed.

The strap on the haversack broke as it was going through customs. We were given our free travel bags and prayer books as we entered the foyer by the representative of Saint Peter's. The bags are soon filled. A quick look around the duty-free shop to pass the waiting time, then a cold drink which goes down well before we board the plane. Stung, not only by an insect on my left wrist (now swollen) while waiting for the coach in London but by the price of the drinks. Ninety-five pence each, forty-four for the milk this morning. Wicked *****! In wandering around the departure lounge we find a free competition to fill in, so enter. I hold Monsieur Lapin in my hand so he can watch the to-ing and fro-ing around us. I had to detach him from the haversack (now mended) as this has to go in the locker above the seats in the plane. I didn't want him squashed.

Our seat numbers were thirteen E and F. Two ten p.m., aboard the plane and seated. We are by a window overlooking the right wing. Seat belts fastened, not many seats empty, I observe. The hostess is speaking over the tannoy, reminding everyone to put hand luggage into the lockers and to leave the passageways and exit doors free. Set for off, ten minutes was all it took to board us all. The wheel bound passengers were catered for first, then us. Well-organized, neat and tidy. Engines are running (I need the loo)) one hour twenty-five minutes is flight time to Lourdes.

We're off along the runway, WHOOSH up in the air, video had been explaining "things" - safety rules and facilities available. Cabin crew check over all of us, safely belted into our seats for take-off. Up and away we zoom into the sky. The houses and scenes below look like dolls' toys, patchwork fields are a picture to behold, God's creation. Through and above the clouds we soar, what a joy, like a dream, Hot meals are being served. Six and a half miles up in the air, flying over a thunderstorm. All food is served with tomato-based substance, poor me !

Desperate for a wee, disturbed our row of people to go - what a relief! Richard is trying out the earphones, radio and TV channels, we have changed seats so he can look below at the views. He has classical music on, *bliss* he says. Oh just found out I should have ordered my food before the flight, never mind, don't like to fuss or to be fussed, will take what comes and eat what I can; I'll not starve. Duty-free drinks, cigarettes, perfume are being sold.

We are descending gradually. Twenty-three degrees centigrade below us, we are told. (Richard is my ears). Gone up two degrees since we left Luton. "Fasten seat belts" the sign says so we all obey, down, down we go, a smooth landing, disembarking is done in double quick time. Maddy and Pat greet us, these are our guides, who sort us out into the waiting coaches, we are the last of three.

Soon at the hotel. *Posh*, our room is on the third floor, twin beds, bath, shower, bidet, scalding hot water, instants when the tap is turned, telephone also, Missing the electric kettle and soap, a must for the English is the cuppa. The view from the window is *rubbish* as we overlook the bins. Dinner, meet other groups, we are the only ones in this hotel from our assigned group so at first feel a little out of things , but soon make new friends and are happy, joining their group.

What a to-do, several of the reps have been to see the manager over the diet folk, the food is done en masse in the kitchen, no joy, so we will have to ad-lib, see what's on our plates we can eat. Each of us stated on our application forms the type of diet we were on. There has been a note in French and English put on my table to remind the waiters of my difficult eating habits, as I had nothing to eat this meal. No tea or coffee is served at the table, all this is extra to be paid for at the bar, so we have a cup of coffee before we retire, as we are both too tired to go to the Grotto for the opening of this pilgrimage. We are in the quiet part of the hotel so should get some sleep tonight in peace.

CHAPTER FIVE

Tuesday - I've had a rough night because of being "poorly", put down to the travelling and no food. However, we are now at the Statue of Our Lady, in front of the Basilica and Domain at eight fifteen a.m. We are going to the new hospital chapel for prayers. Weather is brilliant even at this time of the morning. Some of us are sitting under the trees on the stone seats (cold to the bum), waiting to climb the steep hill to the chapel. Most folk as they pass by us are wearing IDs of their groups, no getting lost here. The steep climb is worth it. The service over, enjoyed it we make our way back to the Domain for a group photo, Toilets here are communal so Richard takes me in as the doors are awkward.

Next on the programme is the Baths. The water is healing water and as I haemorrhaged twice last night I go in Faith to be healed and I am *healed* no sign of blood or discharge when I go to the toilet after. Praise the Lord. Your skin burns after dipping into the healing waters and dries instantly, no need for towels. It a beautiful feeling.

Maddy, bless her, has found a wheel chair for me to use. I'm glad of it's wheels to go "walkies." The sun is blazing down from a cloudless sky, sun hats are fashion just now. Soon we are in the courtyard of Astoria where we stayed last year. An Irish lad told me then I would get well and I did after the operation. The group are to go for a walk around the town visiting the places of Bernadette and her family where they lived and worked. Richard is exploring the hotel shops. Most hotels have shops attached to them at the entrance of the building. Time for me to sit and look, peaceful sitting in the shade.

Off we plod to enjoy our walk with Maddy, telling us the history of the Soubirous family. Most of the places are museums. I'm getting nicely sunburnt in the chair, so is Ann, the other lass having a "push." Richard is a brick to wheel me around in this heat wave, and it is all uphill. My pen has melted in the heat so I will only be able to write at the hotel.

Parish Church is our last viewing, we leave the group here and head for our favourite café for coffee. Ann and John, her pusher, beat us to it. That drink was good, followed by a cold one plus ice cubes, Sheer bliss to the throat. The sky has clouded over while we consumed our drinks so we will go back to the hotel and bathe, change clothes before dinner, a much needed rest for Richard as his feet are sore. A heavy shower empties the streets but fills the shops (good for trade). Cool, cool rain, refreshing the air. I've enjoyed my wheelchair ride.

Some unknown folk at the baths this morning prayed over me when they anoited my ears in the bath, it gave me an uplift of spirit. The day is at an end. Richard asked for hot water at the bar so we've brewed "Bliss." This hotel is named "Paradis" and was only opened at Easter, It certainly is paradise.

CHAPTER SIX

Wednesday, slept fitfully, late, will have to hurry to get our continental breakfast, three different kinds of bread rolls. Weather looks canny outside as we peep out of the windows as we walk down the long corridor to get to the restaurant. On my feet for the morning, to walk down the Grotto area, visiting the crypt and several of the other chapels.

Just sitting within the crypt, quietness brings peace to the soul. We spent time praying then went to the taps to wash and drink, also lit a candle for all pilgrims here and at home. Everyone is a pilgrim. From where we now stand on the steps of the crypt we have a fine view of the river Gave and surrounding area. Thousands of people milling around beneath us at the taps and we listen to the various services in different parts of the "park" attached to the Grotto. Two more films are completed and fresh one put in the cameras for this afternoons tour of the mountains. Sketched three drawing while just reflecting. It is lovely not to rush, rush, but to take time out of the day for quiet.

As I mentioned before each day, we wash and drink at the taps. Suddenly I realize I can hear clear sounds, voices, birds, what a joy, my throat is also better as I can swallow the water today without difficulty. I share this "happening" with Richard.

Monsieur Lapin and the extra Ted I had on me now have a new owner, a little lad who sits at the next table to us in the hotel. He is cute, well-mannered and not a bit of bother. It is a delight to see him so content playing with the toys.

Gavine, this afternoon's tour was pleasant, started from the hotel at on-thirty p.m. on the dot. On the journey various interesting scenery was pointed out to us. Some of the mountains still have snow and it was boiling hot in the coach. Shepherds' huts perched on rocks fascinated us, with small pastures besides for safety of the sheep in bad weather. Some are still is use solidly built of local stone off the mountains, as were the village houses. What a shame to see abandon huts and houses in ruins. Trees

19

and more trees on the mountain slopes, how do they grow from what seems solid rock? Waterfalls cascading down gullies are indescribable, a beautiful, beautiful sight, water generators' stations to harness the water were blended into the scenery. Tourists are well catered for all the year round; we notice the ski lifts and ski runs. I'd love to go to the top of a mountain in one just for the experience and to view the world.

Shower of rain seems to come from nowhere, and the sun still shines. It cools us off and we are not even wet. Wild flowers are in abundance but only to look at - no picking. Let everyone enjoy nature at its best. An earthquake dislodges boulders as big as a house and these form waterfalls which look natural, lovely to sit by, if we had the time to spare. There is so much to see that you can't take it all in.

Richard has bought me to the "Holy Hour" in the chair, it is evening. We are in the upper Basilica and experience an inexplicable "happening". A pool of water forms at the foot of the Statue of our Lady as the service is in progress. The priest in his talk says other denomination did not honour Mary. Without either of us knowing, both Richard and Myself, seeing this "happening" quickly murmur, "We believe." The puddle stops. It looks as if Mary has shed tears. After the service we speak to each other of this "happening"; neither of us likes to dabble a finger in the water to bless ourselves. This as a true experience and written as it happened to two Protestants.

CHAPTER SEVEN

It is another day, Thursday. Spent the morning by going back to the Parish Church, looking at the nearby open market, then sitting a little while by the Garden of Remembrance. We browsed around the souvenir shops. Weather cloudy, clammy, warm, but walkable. The sun also peaked through when we came back to the hotel to rest before lunch. After this, we go to the Grotto: although teeming with people you can sit, reflect and pray, without embarrassment.

Louie (last year's Ted) will be riding with me in the chair, as we join in the afternoon procession with thousands taking part. Richard has to be stern with the beggars bothering us, as the are well-looked after by the village. We are told not give to them, so obey. Although it is crowded here it doesn't feel so. I have noticed many of the bigger hotels have patios on their roofs. I spied on them as I was being pushed down the hill by my wonderful husband, Richard. This chair has been a real boon.

Because of the rain falling gently the service will be in the underground Basilica. Wow, it is hugh, bigger than a football pitch! Claustrophobia is not a problem for both of us as it is "airy", and plenty to observe. I have a front seat, courteous to wheelchairs. It is an international service. Richard has to sit elsewhere in the building , I feel lost without him near me, still, I have a canny view of proceedings. After the Blessing Richard is quick in rescuing me to take us back to the to the hotel for the evening meal.

Going with the crowds we are soon up the hill and in "Paradis." The rain is not much, just enough to cool the air. Money check come next, is almost the end of our pilgrimage. I've noticed the pavement's kerbs in some parts are a bit high, a strain on Richard as he pushes me around. Oh, I make a lovely sound of a car motor horn to get folk to shift themselves out of the way of the chair's wheels, as a knock in the leg will hurt.

Finish our day by having a soft drink plus ice cubes at the bar, it goes down a treat.

CHAPTER EIGHT

Our last day. Six fifteen a.m, we walk to the Grotto for the last time on this pilgrimage. Not surprised to see lots of people about, some are at the taps filling containers to take back home, others like us are sitting, just sitting, quietly and at peace.

Back at breakfast young Daniel, our wee friend, is sad. We explain all holidays have to end. He gave us a gift last night to remember him by; how thoughtful. We've enjoyed the company of all our new friends, some have asked us to keep praying for them when we get home. All rooms must be vacated by eight-thirty a.m., the new pilgrims are coming in as we are leaving, a quick turnover for the hotel staff. Our luggage is kept separate as we are going to Luton, the rest to Gatwick. Richard has returned the wheelchair to Astoria, where it was borrowed from.

The last tour is to the City of the Poor this morning. Louie (Ted) is tucked into the waistband of my slacks. Makes folk smile. What a pleasant surprise to be given an anniversary gift by a new friend. (I'd forgotten all about it - our tenth). A postcard from Spain was also presented to us on our table (nice laddie); this was one tour we were not able to go on. Couldn't do everything.

Richard gives me a fountain pen and a surprise parcel of a shoulder bag. I'd seen in one of the shops earlier in the week , he chose a biro and a candle when we did the last minute shopping before we left the city.

Last weather report: cloudy, cool. Even though it was cloudy, we got sunburnt. I've shared me experience of Monday night when I Haemorrhaged so heavily twice in the night, but was healed instantly when we prayed together. Last year I was so sick with a polyp tumour (operation put me better, remember) that I was depressed. One night I felt myself being lifted from the bed (I was still awake), set in front of a person in white; others like me were also there, we were told to go back to earth as our time had not yet come. Jesus still has work for you to do here on earth, we were told.

Two p.m.: blessing service by the river in front of the Grotto. Daniel and I sit in front of the group with our backs to them. We listen to the service. End of blessing. Little lad upset so ask, "Why?" Reply - he had not been blessed personally, as at nursery school, so we hold our own "blessing". All is still as the little boy puts his hands together and prays aloud the prayer he says at home and in the nursery. What a lovely end to our pilgrimage.